IMAGES OF ENGLAND

NEWTOWN AND SUMMER LANE

IMAGES OF ENGLAND

NEWTOWN AND SUMMER LANE

PETER DRAKE AND JON GLASBY

TEMPUS

Frontispiece: The former generating station in Summer Lane,
photographed by Ray Shill from a barge on the Birmingham
and Fazeley canal in the 1990s. The photograph looks across the
splendid 1842 Barker bridge. The ex-power station is currently
being converted to provide apartment living. In the early nineteenth
century the canal marked the extent of the town's spread from its
centre, later it attracted industry to the district and now it provides
a backdrop to the new generation of urban dwellings which are
transforming many of the city's old commercial buildings.

First published 2006

Tempus Publishing Limited
The Mill, Brimscombe Port,
Stroud, Gloucestershire, GL5 2QG
www.tempus-publishing.com

British Library Cataloguing in Publication Data.
A catalogue record for this book is available from the British Library.

ISBN 0 7524 4197 3

Typesetting and origination by Tempus Publishing Limited.
Printed in Great Britain.

Contents

Acknowledgements

Unless otherwise stated all photographs in this book are from the collection of Birmingham City Council's Central Library. However the authors have used a number of other providers. The photographs in chapter five have been generously made available by the Birmingham Settlement.

The authors are particularly grateful to Nick Hedges for so many powerful images in chapter four taken for the Birmingham Housing Trust and the Royal Town Planning Institute.

The authors are also very grateful to Andy Maxam of Maxam Cards and Kieron McMahon for their help with research on Newtown pubs. Also Ray Shill has helped out through his encyclopaedic knowledge of local industries. Thanks to Desmond Gumbs for permission to use his contemporary photographs - they are credited to Ebenoes.

Last but far from least, the wealth of research and accurate detail which identifies all of the captions to those photographs which feature buses and trams in the area are the work of the transport historian David Harvey. Given that these photographs have also come from David's unrivalled collections the authors owe him a massive debt.

Foreword

See the palm trees swaying way down Summer Lane,
Every Saturday night there's a jubilation,
See the folk's a singing at the 'Salutation',
No snow in Snow Hill,
There's no need to catch a train,
To your southern home where the weather is warm,
It's always summer in Summer Lane.

Written in the early 1920s by two local chaps, Elijah Berry and Howard Gines, as a reaction to the popularity of the songs about 'Dixie' (the southern states of America), 'See the Palm Trees Swaying' was a song about our own home town. Its verses described the city centre but its chorus joyously focused on Summer Lane, the quintessential Brummie working-class street and neighbourhood. London may have had its East End, Glasgow its Gorbals, Dublin its Liberties, Sheffield its Attercliffe, and Liverpool its Scotland Road and they may have been well publicised nationally, but Birmingham had its Summer Lane.

The only part of Birmingham to have its own song, Summer Lane ran the long way uphill from Snow Hill to Asylum Road where Alma Street and Aston began. Packed with shops, factories, workshops, back-to-backs and some better quality houses, it was not just a main road – it gave its name to a neighbourhood that encompassed the streets of Hockley and the Gun Quarter that ran to and from it. And like The Lane itself they have been drawn into stories and legends that abound about Summer Lane. It was reckoned that there was a pub on every corner, but only one on 'The Lane' itself; it was declared that it was the roughest, toughest part of the city down which the coppers had to walk not in twos but in threes; and it was said that Sir Charles Houghton Rafter, the chief constable in the early twentieth century, pronounced that he would so clean up Birmingham that he would be able to hang his fob watch over a lamppost in Summer Lane overnight and pick it up again the next day.

The novel by John Douglas, *A Walk Down Summer Lane*, was seen by many Summer Laners as reinforcing negative stereotypes of the area and it caused a furore when it was published in 1977. Serialised in the *Evening Mail,* it was disliked by many Summer Laners who were angered that it seemed to portray The Lane as a place of squalor, drunken rows, and rough people. In response, Pauline and Bernard Mannion wrote a book called *The Summer Lane and Newtown of the Years between the Wars 1918-1938.* Pauline recognised that 'lots of tales have been told about Summer Lane, some true, some fanciful', but stressed that she and her brother were genuine Summer Laners, 'who want their memories of life in The Lane in the 1920s and 1930s to go on record for all to read about'. Deeply researched and informed by two people who belonged, the Mannions' book recounted the shops and industries of Summer Lane, it recalled everyday life and what children got up to, it highlighted the role of the Settlement, the Copec Housing Society and Bridge Street West Police Station, it encompassed the local cinemas, theatre and dance halls, it drew in High Street Aston and Newtown Row, and it brought to the fore the importance of schools and churches.

The Mannions did not shy away from the problems of drunkenness and violence, but such problems were not confined to Summer Lane and nor indeed were they confined to working-class districts; but most importantly their down-to-earth approach emphasised the neighbourliness of the people of Summer Lane and their pride in their street – qualities which they shared with all those who lived in the poorer working-class neighbourhoods of urban Britain. Summer Laners were not rough: they were rough and ready. Tough they may have been but caring they were too. Bonded together by hard times and shared experiences as much as they were tied by kinship and neighbourliness, the families of Summer Lane are rightly proud of where they come from and to which part of Birmingham they belong. Overlooked in most histories of Birmingham, they even had their name taken away in the post-war redevelopment of Birmingham when the Council renamed the area Newtown. But no-one can take away memories, feelings, and an identity, all of which will be evoked by this new work on Summer Lane and Newtown. The Mannions' book has long been out of print and unavailable. At last another publication asserts the distinctiveness of The Lane.

Professor Carl Chinn MBE

Introduction

You could be forgiven for never realising that Summer Lane and Newtown existed. Open almost any Birmingham history book and the area doesn't features at all – or if it does, it is only included because of the General Hospital it once housed. And yet, Summer Lane is one of the oldest areas of Birmingham, mentioned in documents as far back as 1260. Once a dirt track from Birmingham to Walsall, Summer Lane is rumoured to have earned its name because it was only passable in summer. Although initially housing a few wealthy citizens on the edge of the city, industrialisation and urbanisation meant that Summer Lane quickly became home to large numbers of people, housed in crowded back-to-backs and working in Birmingham's 'thousand trades'. While Summer Lane has always been a poor area, there are very different attitudes to it. Planners and outsiders often saw it as a slum, characterised by poor housing, by heavy drinking and by street fights at closing time. People who lived there recall the hard-working dignity of local people and the communal spirit of the courtyards – poor but happy. It is for this reason that we have decided to compile this book of photographs. Summer Lane is in many ways a typical 'image of England' – working class and poor, but hard-working, dignified and real. If Summer Lane has been edited out of the history of Birmingham, these photographs are intended to put it back on the map and to pay tribute to the lives of the people who lived there.

With so much industry on its doorstep, Summer Lane was badly damaged during the Second World War. However, much more fundamental was the post-war redevelopment of the area, with back-to-backs replaced with tower blocks. In the process, the whole area was redesigned into a series of residential, recreational and industrial zones, and Summer Lane today is now home to workshops and factory units rather than houses. Local families – previously friends and neighbours – were dispersed, often to new estates on the edge of the city, many of which soon experienced as many social problems as before but without the social networks to make the best of them. Even the name of the area was changed (from Summer Lane to Newtown) as part of a newspaper competition to find names for Birmingham's redeveloped areas that would make them sound more modern. Now anyone living in Newtown (or South Aston as it is sometimes called) is likely to be living in high-rise accommodation, separated from other residential areas by open spaces or busy roads. While the standard of new accommodation was better than before, the violence of these changes and the disruption to local neighbourhood life have made many wonder if it was worth it.

Just as the physical infrastructure of Summer Lane has changed, so too has the nature of the local population. Predominantly white until the 1970s, the ethnic make-up of the community has gradually changes with the arrival of Irish, Afro-Caribbean and later Asian settlers. Like many other areas of Birmingham's inner-city, Newtown is now a much more diverse and rich community.

Throughout these changes, a leading Birmingham voluntary organisation – the Birmingham Settlement – has been working from its base on Summer Lane to help meet the needs of local people. Founded in 1899, the Settlement was initially meant to bring together local people with students from Birmingham University and members of some of Birmingham's leading families as a way of promoting friendship and social cohesion. Over time, it has developed into a multi-purpose voluntary organisation and local centre, recently moving from Summer Lane to an annexe in a local tower block. Although the history of the Settlement has been written elsewhere (Glasby, 1999), we are indebted to the Settlement for access to their collection of photographs. Whereas the City Council has many photographs of Summer Lane and Newtown, these are often of buildings and of local houses prior to demolition and it is perhaps a telling sign that the Settlement has more photographs of local people in their own environment. We are grateful to Carl Chinn for his foreword and to Brian Harding from the Summer Lane Society. Finally, for anyone wanting some personal memories of Summer Lane, we recommend the accounts provided by Pauline and Bernard Mannion (1985, 1987), which serve as a more detailed and colourful commentary to accompany this book. Above all, we hope we do justice to an area that many people love and still identify with and which was a core part of making Birmingham the city it is today.

The books listed below have greatly helped with research for this book:

Glasby, J. (1999) *Poverty and opportunity: one hundred years of the Birmingham Settlement*. Studley, Brewin Books.
Mannion, P. and Mannion, B. (1985) *The Summer Lane and Newtown of the years between the wars, 1918-1938*. Birmingham, Mannion and Mannion.
Mannion, P. and Mannion, B. (1987) *Pub memories of Summer Lane and Newtown between the wars*. Birmingham, Mannion and Mannion.
An extremely good and useful website is www.astonbrook-through-astonmanor.co.uk

one

Local
Landmarks

Above and below: Two old engravings of the General Hospital when it was in Summer Lane. It was the first hospital in Birmingham and was the main landmark in the district until its demolition in 1901.

Opposite: Dr John Ash, the main founder of the General Hospital. A very familiar and well-connected surgeon in the town in the middle of the eighteenth century, Dr Ash became concerned at the increasing number of industrial accidents taking place as Birmingham entered the industrial revolution. At the time Birmingham was still a relatively small town with a population of 35,000, so the lack of a hospital was not that evident. Dr Ash placed an advertisement in the local newspaper in November 1765 calling a meeting to build a 'General Hospital for the relief of the Sick and Lame.' In this portrait Dr Ash looks to perfection 'the doctor' as tradition and literature has handed down.

Thomas Lewis took this photograph of the General Hospital not long before the new General Hospital was built in Steelhouse Lane to replace the Summer Lane buildings. A contemporary description of the hospital in the 1890s described 'the only oasis in Summer Lane was the General Hospital which stood serene and sedate with its Greek portico under which the lame and the maimed were continually passing. Always there seemed to be a steady stream of men and women, some on stretchers, often begrimed with marks of their occupation in the numerous metal trades of the city'

The General Hospital's dispensary in 1897. The hospital was extended on several occasions during its life and the dispensary was added as part of extensive alterations in 1857.

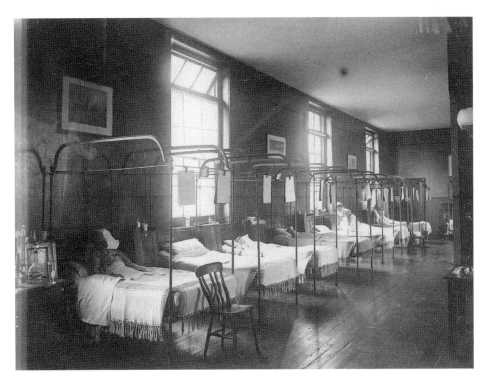

Above: Ward six, photographed by Howard Collins. The General Hospital opened with only forty beds rather than the 100 planned but it greatly expanded over the years to cater for the town's rapidly increasing population and its attendant unsafe industries.

Below: The House Governors sitting room in the 1890s.

Left: 'Granny', formerly a housemaid at the General Hospital, for years supplied newspapers and magazines to the patients.

Below: The Birmingham Civic Society's blue plaque on the Metro building commemorating the site of the original General Hospital. (Ebenoes)

The mortuary on the corner of Summer Lane and Henrietta Street in 2006. Internally the building consisted of three recesses where bodies could be laid out and at the back there was a garden for members of the public to sit. The mortuary was used for deaths of residents of the Model Lodging House nearby and in any of the surrounding courts. A feature on the building appeared in the trade journal *The Architect and Building News* in May 1933. The building is now a private residence with its entrance in Henrietta Street. (Ebenoes)

St George's church, the district's premier church, situated at the corner of Great Hampton Row and Tower Street. It was built on green fields and the Bishop of Chester, when consecrating the building in 1822, expressed his surprise that it was built so far from any people. However, within a year, so fast was the speed of building, that it was surrounded by the new town.

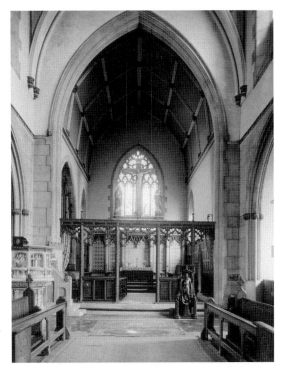

Right: St George's was the architect Thomas Rickman's first building in Birmingham. Rickman is best known for his pioneering work on English Gothic architecture and his interests and work came together in the design of St George's church.

Below: St George's churchyard on a summer's day in 1979, an oasis of peace in the middle of an inner city suburb. Thomas Rickman was buried in the churchyard in a tomb with a suitably gothic arched canopy.

A view of St George's taken in 1901 by George Whitehouse. The tower was visible for miles around, making the church the district's most visible landmark.

The Tower Street elevation of St George's, filmed on 7 April 1954.

Sadly, and rather surprisingly, the church wasn't spared in the wholesale redevelopment of the district and here the bulldozers are at work on 3 November 1960.

Above: St George's Rectory House on New John Street West in December 1956.

Opposite below: The Evangelical Mission in Ormond Street on 7 December 1956, backing onto the Coleshill Place courts off Cowper Street. Officially called the Free Church of England Mission, it had been dedicated in 1933 and had a strong Band of Hope influence. There were numerous missions and chapels in the area, many of which saw themselves in opposition to the even more numerous pubs and drinking houses for which Newtown was renowned. In reality the missions did considerable work in helping to alleviate the appalling conditions which surrounded them.

Right: The People's Chapel in Great King Street. Built on the site of an 1841 chapel which was destroyed by fire in 1887, the People's Chapel took a leading role in the 1930s in 'mission work' to the newly built estates on the fringes of the city.

One of the new schools built in Newtown when the area was redeveloped, Brearley Street school in January 1964.

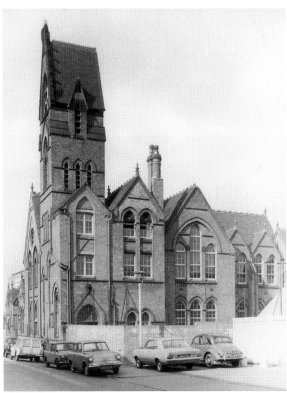

Above: William Cowper School was one of the prominent Board schools that catered for the impoverished children of Newtown – indeed, William Cowper School was said to take the poorest children of all. The school was opened in 1885 and built by the firm of Martin and Chamberlain, the Birmingham architects who designed so many of the Victorian schools, with their very distinctive architecture.

Left: Smith Street School, another Victorian Board school just on the edge of Newtown. Opened in 1876 it was designed to take nearly a thousand pupils.

Above and below: An old Georgian house numbered 381 Summer Lane at the corner with Hospital Street. For many years it was used as a doctor's surgery as in the above photograph taken in 1932, when the doctor was Dr Orton. He was well known for travelling on his rounds on a pony and trap or an old bike and carrying a Gladstone bag. The Model Lodging House next door was locally known as the doss house and was a sanctuary to homeless and usually unemployed men in the 1930s. An entertaining account of trying to take the census in 1891 at the Model Lodging House appears in the book *Less Paint, More Vanity* by A. Matthison, himself the son of the local registrar of births, marriages and deaths who lived at that time next door in the old Georgian house. 'Of course the bulk of the information and names were false and most men made their mark. No names, no pack drill'. Fun for the modern family historian. The lower photograph shows the house in disrepair in August 1947 and it was subsequently demolished.

The MEB building in Summer Lane is one of the real landmarks at the beginning of The Lane coming from town. As part of the city's municipalisation programme (privatisation in reverse) the city purchased the Birmingham Electric Supply Co. in 1899. Recognizing the need to increase electricity supply capacity the city bought the site of the old General Hospital for a new generating station. This opened on 10 October 1906 with a larger capacity than originally planned in order to cope with the recent expansion of the city's tramway system. The engine room was large enough to have housed the Town Hall. It was here in August 1923 that the BBC began transmitting wireless programmes with the call sign 5 IT.

Opposite, above and below: The Colmore estate dwellings were designed by the architect Arthur Harrison and built as model accommodation for 'the proper housing of Birmingham's working class population'. This tenement was built around 1900 to improve the local housing standards and it contained twenty-three flats on four storeys. Such tenement housing never really caught on in Birmingham so this building is important both socially and architecturally. The block was designed with its own integral shop to act like a village store. Unfortunately the building is not now in the best state of repair as the contemporary photograph shows. (Ebenoes)

Bridge Street West police station in 2006. The current police station was built in 1939 and the city's coat of arms sits proudly over the entrance. It replaced the earlier one which occupied two cottages further down the street. Before the war and immediately after it there was no denying that Newtown and Summer Lane had a 'reputation' and there was no arguing with the fact that the station was needed. Saturday night fights, illegal betting and other crimes were a constant fact of life in the crowded streets. Police responses were different in those days: a correspondent to one of the Birmingham papers in November 1939 looked back fondly on an even earlier date. Commenting on the death of an old Summer Lane policeman Jimmy Walters the writer paid tribute to 'Jimmy's wonderful pluck and fistic prowess. I also recall his numerous off duty periods to repair his broken fists and his unconventional shirtsleeve tussles round Harding Street, long since changed to Moorsom Street'. (Ebenoes)

Opposite above: Newman's factory in Hospital street. William Newman and Sons were manufacturers of door closers and floor springs whose products are found in virtually every country of the world. Summer Laners recall that getting a job at Newman's was justly regarded as real feather in your cap.

Another massive works, the gun and pistol manufactory of Bentley and Playfair on Summer Lane, just a mile or so away from the city's gun quarter. In 1868 it advertised itself as ' Manufacturers of Every Description of Military and Sporting Rifles, Guns, Pistols and Revolvers and of the Most Improved Breech Loaders…..Contractors to Her Majesty's War Department'.

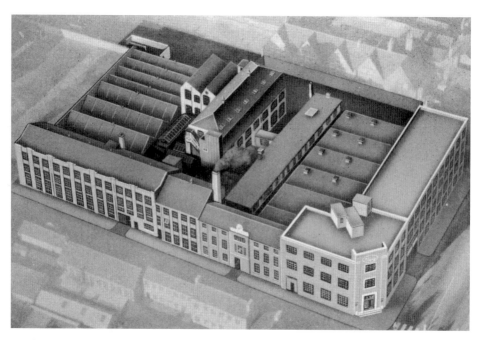

Above and below: The head office and Brearley Street factory of Newey Brothers. The district has always had a strong industrial presence; in the past this included many world famous Birmingham names though more recently most of the very large factories have proved surplus to requirements and instead smaller units and workshops dominate. The Newey's building was erected around 1840 and is Grade II listed. The company were awarded a royal warrant after providing the hooks and eyes which were used on Queen Mary's coronation robes in 1911.

two

Pubs

The architectural jewel in Newtown is the Bartons Arms. The Bartons Arms public house, standing in the angle between High Street, to the left, and Potters Lane on the right still stands today and is regarded as architecturally one of the best suburban public houses in England.

Above and right: Replacing a previous tavern which had been built in 1840, the Bartons Arms was designed by the James and Lister Lea Co. in a mock-Jacobean style for the Mitchells and Butlers brewery and opened in 1901. With its terracotta brickwork, Minton tiling, relief ceilings and snob screens, the inside of the Bartons Arms is quite stunning. Although a few years ago it was in danger of closure the pub is now a thriving real ale house which adds to its appeal by providing a unique Thai food menu.

The Green Man at the corner of Summer Lane and Moorsom Street photographed shortly before the pub closed in March 1965. At the time the licensee was Frederick Holland. (Andrew Maxam)

Nearly every pub featured here is a corner pub. This one, The Rose and Crown, was on the corner of Brearley and Hospital Streets and this is how it looked on 27 January 1963 as the area around it was demolished. It was to close a few months later. The pub had been badly damaged during a wartime air raid. Customers who had been using the cellars as a shelter were rescued along with, according to local gossip, plenty of barrels which ended up in nearby houses for 'safe keeping'. (Andrew Maxam)

This is another well-remembered but now demolished corner pub, the Birmingham House, at the corner of Summer Lane and Farm Street, seen here in March 1968. This pub also suffered during the war – two young men who were fire watching on the roof were killed by an incendiary bomb. At one time the pub opened in the early mornings to provide market workers with rum and coffee on their way to work.

A corner pub which survived the redevelopment was, and is, the Royal George. This is the first pub you come to if you start from town along Summer Lane, on the William Street North corner. One of the first pubs in Newtown, at one time, the licensee was the ex-Birmingham City and England goalkeeper from the 1930s, Dick Tremelling. Ex-footballers and particularly old boxers made up a high proportion of landlords in the inter-war years. (Andrew Maxam)

Newtown had two Salutation pubs. This is the one in Alma Street but the best known, and the one which is refereed to in the poem quoted above in the introduction, was the other one. The Summer Lane Salutation, a large Victorian building, was itself a replacement for an eighteenth-century pub. It was a rather grand building with its own gardens and bowling green and until the district was built up was regarded as a country pub. It dominated the Summer Lane-Snow Hill corner. At the turn of the last century another ex-footballer, the Aston Villa star Dennis Hodgetts, ran the Salutation. Unfortunately, it was once reported in a Villa programme, all his medals were stolen from behind the bar.

The brilliantly named Cottage of Content, seen here in 1903. Situated in Newtown Row, opposite St Stephen's church hall, it was a small pub with a step down to the bar.

Above and below: Two views of the Stags Head in Summer Lane on the corner with Brearley Street, one of the few pubs to survive the redevelopment of the area. It was well known at one time for being the only pub in the area with a 'Men Only' bar. Ladies were only allowed to use a small portioned-off section of the bar. The lower photo shows the pub decked out with bunting supporting England in the 2006 World Cup. (Andrew Maxam; Ebenoes)

As well as corner pubs, Newtown also boasted a number of small pubs tucked among shops. The Clement Arms on Newtown Row still survives but this pub, The British Lion, also on Newtown Row, was demolished. This is how it looked on 23 July 1959, at 11.25 a.m. if the garage clock was accurate.

Opposite above: The Woodman, the last pub from town in Summer Lane on the corner with Asylum Road, better known as The Wrexham, an Atkinson's house selling Wrexham ales. It also had a reputation in the 1930s as a 'strap shop', somewhere you could buy a pint of cider at 3d a pint on the slate. (Andrew Maxam)

Opposite below: A 'survivor'. The White Horse on the corner of Newtown Row and New John Street West was popular with cinemagoers from the Newtown Palace across the road.

Above: There were a number of off-licences, or 'offies', in the district as well and here is one on the corner of Porchester and Denmark Streets photographed on 23 January 1968. Margaret Bailey was the licencee.

Left: The Brook Tavern on Lennox Street on 17 November 1966. All the pubs in the area tended to have a reputation for Saturday night violence, right up to the 1960s. One of Newtown's most prominent sons, the trade union leader and MP Will Thorne, recalls in his autobiography, 'drinking and fighting should not be magnified. We were healthy normal human beings, fond of fair play, we had little amusement and little opportunity to enjoy the better things in life'.

Right: The Duke of Cambridge at 150–151 Great King Street on the corner with Berners Street. (Andrew Maxam)

Below: The Fountain Inn, an Ansells pub, at 327 Farm Street, August 1961.

The Sportsmans Inn on the corner of Moosom Street and Newtown Row, one of the last of the Newtown pubs to be closed in 1973. It was built before 1865. A nineteenth-century observer reported that in the working-class areas of the city, like Newtown, 'the publicans and spirit dealers are the only class of the community that provide that light sort of entertainment which is as necessary to health as rest and sleep are to the body'.

On the corner of Brearley Street and Great Hampton Row, the Star and Garter pub was remembered in the inter-war years as a very lively house, running a range of angling, domino and football clubs. Its upstairs room was used for wedding receptions. This view shows how the pub looked on 24 November 1960. The newsagent carries advertisements for the *News of the World's* serialisation of Sophia Loren's autobiography and a poster, 'He is coming', promoting an Oswald Mosley meeting at the Town Hall. Mosley had been a prominent political figure in the city in the 1920s even though his Blackshirts never achieved much local support in the 1930s and his meetings after the war were pretty tame by comparison with the pre-war ones.

The Geach Arms, on the corner of Summer Lane and Geach Street, August 1961. In the early 1900s there were over a hundred pubs and more than thirty off-licences in and around the Summer Lane district, with one pub for every seventy-seven yards of street space around Newtown Row.

The Vine, Summer Lane, July 1961. By one of those strange quirks, The Vine was the only pub of the Summer Lane establishments to actually have Summer Lane as its postal address in the 1930s; all the others took their address from the adjacent corner street.

The Three Horseshoes, on the corner of Summer Lane with Cowper Street, August 1961. Arrests for drunkenness in the district on the eve of the First World War were about the highest in the city.

The Porchester Arms in Porchester Street on 4 August 1961.

The Scotch House at No. 73 High Street Aston at the corner with Whitehead Street, also on 4 August 1961. The City Planning Department recorded most of the pubs in the area prior to demolition and the redevelopment of Newtown.

The Dolphin, an Ansells house, on the corner of Frankfort Street and Hospital Street in July 1961.

Above: The Bulls Head, Hatchett Street, just down from Summer Lane. Mary Parsons was the licensee in February 1959 when this photograph was taken.

Opposite above: The Barrel Inn on the corner of Summer Lane and Tower Street opposite the Birmingham Settlement. One of the Summer Lane survivors, the Barrel had once been called the Boy in the Barrel. It is recalled as a favourite with youngsters from The Settlement on the other corner of Tower Street and Summer Lane, gaining some Dutch courage before trying their luck at a local Saturday night hop.

Opposite below: Little Brown Jug on Great Hampton Row. With the redevelopment of the district nearly all the local pubs went as well so new 1960s-style pubs were built to replace them.

The Lamplighter in Summer Lane decked out with England flags for the 2006 World Cup.

The Griffin, part of the Newtown Shopping Centre, ironically now demolished, while in the background The Bartons Arms across the road goes from strength to strength, in its second century.

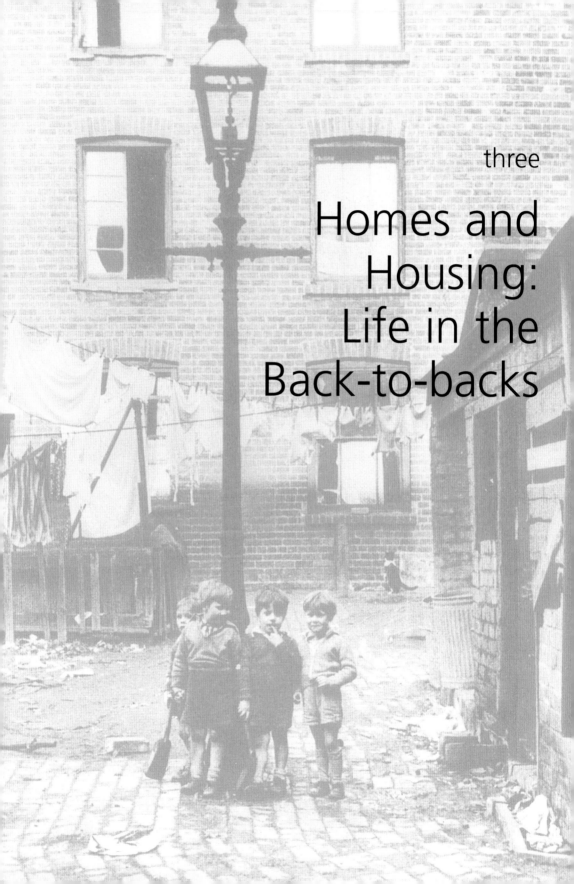

three

Homes and Housing: Life in the Back-to-backs

A group of children in a Summer Lane courtyard, *c.* 1920. At this time, most of Summer Lane consisted of 'back-to-backs', often built in the early nineteenth century when the city's population and industries were rapidly expanding. Typically, these consisted of a double row of houses built literally back-to-back under a single roof. An 'entry' took you into a communal courtyard behind, with communal water closets and a washhouse (or 'brewhouse'). (Courtesy of Birmingham Lives Archive)

Court 21 (Nos 15-17) on Hospital Street. Based near people's places of work the back-to-backs were cheap to rent but were often badly built, in a poor state of repair and usually overcrowded.

Housing of the 1930s. Most houses had one room on each floor and were two- or three-storeys high, with a kitchen on the ground floor, a bedroom above and perhaps an attic. Note in this picture how white the washing looks in the background.

Houses at the rear. Although local bye-laws of 1876 prohibited the building of back-to-backs, they continued to be the norm until well into the twentieth century. By 1913, a Special Housing Committee found some 200,000 people living in back-to-backs, with some Birmingham wards made up of around 50-75 per cent of this type of housing.

No. 14 Thomas Street, Court 9, 1870s. The Housing Committee also found that large numbers of homes had no separate water supply, sinks or drains, concluding that 'a large proportion of the poor in Birmingham are living under conditions of housing detrimental to both health and morals.'

Right: Houses on Unett Street, photographed by the Public Works Department. While many photographs are available of the Summer Lane area, more focus on housing than on local people and were taken by the local authorities as a prelude to redevelopment and 'slum clearance'.

Below: Court 29, Hospital Street. Although the courtyard here looks forbidding, many local people recount how such areas became the focal point for the local community with neighbours knowing each other well and helping each other with child care and in difficult times.

A courtyard on Gee Street, c. 1965. For many local children, the courtyards were also the main space for recreation and play – even if it was jumping the puddles and chasing the pigeons as seems to be the case in this picture. (Courtesy of Birmingham Lives Archive)

No. 50 Brearley Street and an entrance to a court.

Nos 2-8 Brearley Street. Despite poor conditions, a major sign of respectability was the cleanliness of the front of the house – particularly the front step and the net curtains.

Inside a house on Gee Street, *c.* 1920. Note the washing drying over the grate as well as the hole in the ceiling.

Opposite above: Court No. 16 Court on Brearley Street. Part of Birmingham's rapidly expanding inner-city, Summer Lane was home to a large number of houses, but also to many shops, factories and businesses, often all interspersed.

Opposite below: Court No. 1, 4 Unett Street, 1959. This is a photograph of 'sub-standard houses' taken by the City Engineer and Surveyor. Again, note how white the washing is, in contrast with some of the surrounding houses. In the corner is the Unett General Engineering Co.

New Summer Street, 1943. Taken by the City of Birmingham Estates Department, this is a photograph labelled as a representation of housing 'unfit for human habitation'.

Court 17, Hospital Street. While most of the children are wearing boots, two smaller children at the front are bare foot.

No. 221 and Court 29, Hospital Street. Birmingham has long been associated with Quaker and other Non-Conformist leading families (see Chapter six on the Birmingham Settlement), and this shop is selling several products associated with Quaker businessmen and philanthropists, including Fry's Cocoa and Colman's Mustard. Other brands, like R. White's lemonade, continue to be sold to this day.

four

Homes and Housing: Post-war Redevelopment

Above: Repairing war damage on Bridge Street West, 1942. During the Second World War, 2,000 tons of bombs were dropped on Birmingham, causing some 4,863 fires and destroying 12,391 houses. Summer Lane was particularly badly hit because of its proximity to the Lucas factory and other firms involved in producing munitions.

Left: The tower blocks go up. Even more fundamental to change than bomb damage was the clearance of large swathes of inner-city back-to-backs and their replacement with new tower blocks, some in Newtown as tall as twenty storeys high.

Moving out prior to slum clearance, 1967. Summer Lane was one of five post-war redevelopment areas. With its name changed to Newtown, it was based on neighbourhoods of around 10,000 people, with the area divided into a series of residential, recreational and industrial 'zones'. This and several other photographs in this chapter were taken by Nick Hedges as part of projects for the Birmingham Housing Trust (1967) and for the Royal Town Planning Institute (1975). The latter took a critical look at Britain's cities and was used subsequently at the Institute of Contemporary Arts in London.

Above: The Perry Barr Expressway, reservation south of Asylum Road, 1967. As part of the new design, the 'zones' were separated from each other by large open spaces or by new and busy roads that continue to dissect the area to this day.

Above: Building the new tower blocks, 1967. The redevelopment was the brainchild of Herbert Manzioni (City Engineer and Surveyor), who believed passionately in the need to improve the quality of Birmingham's housing stock and designed the new redeveloped areas as a means of improving the quality of life of local people. (Nick Hedges)

Opposite below: Nos 33-53 New Street, 1967. While the redevelopment was planned and implemented, the old continued to coexist with the new. Note here the broken, boarded windows in the foreground, with the new tower block going up in the background.

Above: Perry Barr Expressway, at the corner of Ormond Street and Newtown Row, 1966. In many ways, the car speeding past is an indication of things to come, as Newtown today is dominated almost entirely by the trunk routes that run through it, with friends and neighbours divided by major roads.

Left: Uxbridge Street, 1966. Here you can see boarded-up low-level homes in the background, the new tower blocks and a recreational area in the front.

A rehoused family by their new flat, 1967. Although the tower blocks have since been criticized they were initially much better than what had gone before. In this photograph the smiling faces capture the sense of hope and optimism for a better future. (Nick Hedges)

School play time, 1975. While areas such as this made Newtown much less built-up and more green than before, many were simply open spaces with minimal recreational facilities and later became 'no go' areas as the community changed and crime increased.

Low-rise housing. Between the tower blocks came new low-level housing and small estates.

Newtown children's play area, 1975. After all the initial optimism, a backlash quickly began against the redevelopment. In particular, the tower blocks were seen as having broken up previously tight-knit communities and isolating people from their neighbours. Maintaining the flats was also expensive and their condition quickly deteriorated. (Nick Hedges)

After school, 1967. Despite Manzioni's commitment to recreational 'zones', most inner-city areas have lacked meaningful recreational facilities and activities. Throughout this period, the voluntary agencies that worked in Newtown sought to provide leisure and recreational opportunities for young people at risk of widespread boredom and alienation. (Nick Hedges)

Above: New flats, 1967. As the housing stock has deteriorated, other factors (economic recession, crime, unemployment and poverty) have combined to make Newtown one of Birmingham's most deprived areas. (Nick Hedges)

Left: Gee Street, 1967. When one compares the old back-to-backs with the new tower blocks, one wonders how much has really changed, and whether modern housing in Newtown was any more desirable than that of the late nineteenth century. While the physical infrastructure of the area has changed, numerous underlying problems remain.

Newtown Shopping Centre, 1975. Nowhere is the changing nature of Newtown more apparent than in the fate of the shopping centre, which was initially a focal point of the community and had one of the first Sainsbury's stores in the city. The smiling faces in this poster give a sense of happiness and optimism, emphasizing the importance of 'all your favourite shops in one exciting centre'. (Nick Hedges)

Newtown Shopping Centre. By 1995, only 7 out of 120 units were occupied and the area was known as 'little Beirut' because of the large number of burnt-out cars and frequent muggings. In all the regeneration work that took place during the 1990s, the shopping centre came top of people's list of priorities.

Newtown Shopping Centre. During the 1990s, a £16 million refurbishment led to new office accommodation, the closure of dangerous and dark underpasses and the arrival of new shops such as Aldi, Farmfoods and McDonalds. Even with these changes, it remains to be seen whether this investment will be enough to overcome the long-standing difficulties which Newtown has faced.

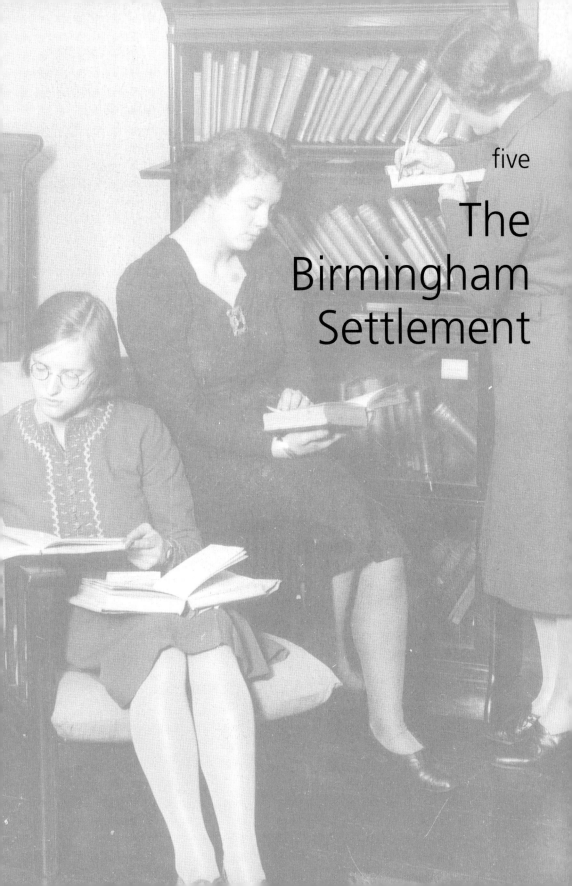

five

The Birmingham Settlement

Above and below: The Birmingham Settlement, No. 318 Summer Lane, 1929. Founded on 29 September 1899, the Settlement was part of a national network of Settlement houses or University Settlements. Beginning in 1884 with the foundation of Toynbee Hall in London, Settlements were colonies of educated people living in large houses in poor areas of large cities. By becoming both friends and neighbours to the poor, these 'settlers' hoped to share the benefits of their education, but also to learn about the realities of poverty at first hand. For all the model was so full of class patronage, prominent settlers include figures such as Clement Attlee and William Beveridge, who used their Settlement experience to introduce major social reform.

Settlers working and resting. From the beginning, Birmingham was one of a number of Women's
Settlements, staffed by female students and workers, and working primarily with local women and
children. Initially the 'Birmingham Women's Settlement', it changed its name to 'Birmingham Settlement'
in 1919 in recognition of increasing work with men and boys.

Above: Midland Red buses taking the mother's group to a garden party – presumably at the house of a wealthy Settlement supporter. From an early stage, offering meaningful recreation was a key part of the Settlement's work and much of the first half of the twentieth century was spent in providing a wide range of educational and leisure activities. For this reason, most of the photographs in this chapter focus on the Settlement's recreational work, although its many other projects have been described in detail elsewhere by Glasby.

Opposite below: Summer Lane, *c.* 1930. Prior to redevelopment, the Settlement was located at the heart of the community it sought to serve, and many local people recall how their lives were entangled with the Settlement – receiving support in a crisis, attending one of the many projects or clubs, meeting a future wife or husband at the Settlement. When the area was redeveloped, the Settlement was initially left isolated in the middle of an industrial zone with no community around it.

Right: Putting up notices on Monday morning, 1931. This tree outside the Settlement was for many years described as being one of the few pieces of greenery in Summer Lane.

Below: A Provident collector visiting Brearley Street. One of the Settlement's first and longest projects was a Provident Society or Penny Bank, encouraging local people to save small sums for future periods of difficulty. Beginning in 1899 with ninety-two houses in Lower Tower Street, the Society soon had branches in five factories, was visiting eleven districts and received around £700 per annum courtesy of some 17,682 deposits. In the end, the Provident Society continued till 1954, and more recent Settlement projects (a money advice centre, a credit union) continue this work to this day.

The Junior Gym Club, 1931.

The Junior Gym Club in the playground.

Waiting to get in, 1932. By the late 1930s, there were some thirty clubs at the Settlement, with boy's clubs, girl's clubs, men's clubs, women's clubs, parties, holidays, sports teams, drama groups, bands and orchestras. Initially focusing on girls and women, the Settlement enlisted male workers from 1912 and began to develop specialist activities for boys. As these young people grew older, the Settlement began to develop more and more work with local men.

Above and left: Work and play at the Boy's Club. By the 1930s, the boy's club had developed into a variety of activities, including football, boxing, carpentry, singing and play writing. There was even a jazz band, described by one observer as consisting of 'seven combs, twelve trombones made out of cardboard, mouth organs, bones for castanets, two violins, a biscuit tin for a drum, a piano of sorts, plus several piercing human whistles!'

The Junior Girl's Club, 1933. This was one of the first Settlement projects, beginning in 1899 for older children about to leave school. With the acquisition of 317 Summer Lane, the scheme quickly expanded to six nights a week, offering activities such as cooking, writing, painting, singing and needlework.

Mother's Club Holiday, 1947. Beginning with a series of 'at home' events with 'conversation, reading, recitations, music, etc', the Settlement's work with women quickly developed into an ongoing series of events and clubs. By the end of the Second World War, many club members were ageing, and the Settlement became increasingly involved in developing new community-based services for older people, such as a day centre, a visiting service and meals-on-wheels.

Extract from a Birmingham Settlement scrapbook, 1930.

Club activities. Soon the Settlement had developed teams in football, netball, cricket, badminton and tennis. As their reputation grew, the cricketers played at the Warwickshire County Ground, while the footballers played in a competition in Spain.

Opening of the Junior Block, 1940. Pictured from left to right are Mr Warren, Mr Ashford, the Lord Mayor and Lady Mayoress, Mr Walker and the Settlement warden, Miss Truscott.

Above and below: The Birmingham Settlement, 2006. In 1932, the Rotary Club paid for a new hall, opened by Sir Austen Chamberlain. The motto – Service above Self – is that of the Rotary Club. After the Settlement's centenary in 1999, the Settlement has taken a new direction and has recently moved from its buildings on Summer Lane to an annexe at nearby Reynolds House. As part of this process, the Settlement is now smaller in size and closer once again to the community it aims to serve. (Ebenoes)

six

A Trip Along Newtown Row and High Street Aston

Above and below: The humped-back bridge over the Birmingham and Fazeley Canal marked the northern end of Lancaster Street and the start of Newtown Row. In the top photograph the motorcyclist overtaking ex-CBT bogie tramcar 451 appears to be taking his life in his hands on the blind bridge. It is December 1949 and the tram has only days left in service before the closure of the Perry Barr tram route on New Year's Eve. On the crest of the canal bridge alongside the tram is a cast-iron urinal, which always seemed to be an ideal place for it! (R.T. Wilson)

On Saturday 31 December 1949, the second of the two former City of Birmingham Tramways eight-wheeled tramcars, 452, was on its last day in service. It was built by that company as an open-top car numbered 180 in 1903 and rebuilt in 1926 with vestibules, direct stairs and a top cover and the huge seating capacity of seventy-one. It is climbing up the hill towards the bridge over the Birmingham and Fazeley Canal as it heads into the city when working on the 6 route from Perry Barr. Alongside the tram on the right is the Globe Works of Henry Wiggins & Co., who were nickel manufacturers and whose main factory was in Wiggin Street, off Icknield Port Road. (F.N. Lloyd Jones)

The Midland Red bus is about to crest the Birmingham and Fazeley Canal bridge when coming into Birmingham on the 188 route from the large, 1930s-built Beeches housing estate. The bus is 4403, (VHA 403), a BMMO D7 fitted with a Metro-Cammell H37/26R body and dating from 1954. The Midland Red bus route 188 was taken over by Birmingham City Transport on 1 September 1957 just a few weeks before 4403 was found travelling to the then City terminus in New Street near to the Odeon Cinema. On the left is the Globe Works factory of Henry Wiggins. Immediately behind the distant Riley Pathfinder car is the almost ogee-shaped corner tower of the Marquis of Lorne public house which was on the corner of Cecil Street. Beyond that is another Midland Red double-decker while a Corporation bus is working on the 33 route to Kingstanding. (A.B. Cross)

Newtown Row showing the shops between Cecil Street and Cliveland Street around 1914. Among the shop fronts covering Nos 26 to 38 was the birdcage manufacturer Henry Chapman at No. 32. He made those old-fashioned cages for canaries out of wood with bars and a feeding trough at the front. He was still trading there in the 1930s.

Looking back towards the city and the bridge over the Birmingham and Fazeley Canal on 21 June 1978 reveals Newtown Row to be in a sorry state. Vast swathes of Newtown Row's Victorian housing was being demolished at the time. At No. 73 Newtown Row, a few yards behind the city-bound bus, was William Shillock's boot and shoe shop, from where, on Thursday 12 September 1895, the original FA Cup was stolen. It had been out on display there after Aston Villa beat West Bromwich Albion 1-0 in the final. It was never seen again. About to pass the entrance to Lower Tower Street on the left is a former Birmingham City Transport Daimler Fleetline 3648, (JOB 648E), on the 52 route to the Beeches Estate, off Walsall Road between Perry Barr and Great Barr. Travelling into Birmingham is one of the two hundred Bristol VRTSL6Gs fitted with Metro-Cammell bodywork. The very square-looking rear engine bustle gave them a somewhat ungainly rear aspect. The bus is one of Birchills garage's allocation and is probably working on the 51 route from Walsall. Both buses are being operated by West Midlands PTE. (E.V. Trigg)

Newtown has two main claims to fame in the history of football in this country. One is the theft of the FA Cup, which has always led locally to the jibe that the Villa have lost the FA cup more times than the Blues have won it. The other connection is with William McGregor who gave his name to the football advertised here. McGregor, the driving force behind the creation of the Football League, owned a drapery business in Summer Lane.

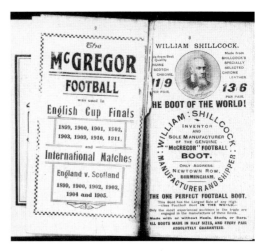

Travelling towards Six Ways along Newtown Row are two buses operating on the 33 route to Kingstanding. The buildings along this section of Newtown Row were already derelict and awaiting demolition. The only identifiable building is one last occupied by Frank Ash, who had advertised his business as 'The Noted Bacon Shop'. When the Perry Barr tramway route was abandoned on New Year's Eve 1949, the 33 bus route was diverted from the former route by way of Newtown Row. The leading bus is 2128, (JOJ 128), which was a 'new-look fronted' Daimler CVD6 with a Metro-Cammell body which had entered service on 1 July 1951 but because of its rather oil-thirsty Daimler CD6 type engine, it was withdrawn fifteen years later. It has just overtaken a 1956 Standard Vanguard III and is being followed by a Triumph Herald convertible. Catching up with the leading bus is a two years older 1701, (HOV 701), a Brush-bodied Leyland Titan PD2/1 which was eventually withdrawn in November 1968. Both buses were allocated to Perry Barr garage. (D.R. Harvey Collection)

Located on the opposite corner of Manchester Street was the Newtown branch of the Birmingham Municipal Bank. The first Municipal Bank was opened on 1 September 1919 and by 1935 there were fifty-seven branches within the city, which included the one in Newtown Row. Although this branch was on the ground floor of a mid-Victorian building, its doorway and frontages were in the Art Deco house style of the bank. Being followed by a pre-war Fordson semi-forward control 2-ton van and a 1940 Fordson Thames 7V 3-ton lorry is BCT tramcar 8. This is one of only six of the twenty BCT bogie cars of 1904 which survived the bombing of Witton and Miller Street depots in December 1940 and April 1941. It is travelling into the city on the 6 route from Perry Barr in about 1949. (F.W. Ivey)

A group of shops at Nos 113 to 117 Newtown Row between Pritchett Street and New John Street in 1898. Here were Henry Wilks and Co, (working cutlers), James Hardstaff, (linen drapers) and the glaziers, Morralls.

Newtown Row premises Nos 92 to 106, between Hatchett Street and Brearley Street, around 1914.

This photograph is from around 1955. Wilson's furniture store on the corner of Newtown Row and New John Street West is selling second-hand furniture as well as brand new items. In the distance, in New John Street, are the grim three-storied walls of back-to-back houses. The bus emerging from New John Street West is 2430, (JOJ 430), one of Liverpool Street garage's early allocation of 'new look' front Crossley DD42/6s with Crossley H30/24R bodies which entered service on 1 June 1950 and lasted until October 1969. It is working on the 19 City Circle route which served the markets and industrial areas at the edge of the city centre such as Digbeth, the Jewellery Quarter and the inner parts of Aston. The 19 service was introduced on 2 March 1932, though because of the war-time service cutbacks which were implemented on 25 September 1939, the service only ran during peak hours of weekdays. (R.F. Mack)

In the early post-war years, Newtown Row had seen better days with some of the worst back-to-back houses in the Birmingham area. Between Newtown Row and Summer Lane to the west and from Cecil Street in the south to Gerrard Street in the north there was some of the most tightly packed and unhygienic housing imaginable. On this gloomy day in about 1948, tramcar 583 stands just beyond the road junction with New John Street West. When new in 1914, this tram was one of six bogie cars to be employed, with added carpeting, cushions and curtains, on the experimental Hagley Road 'First Class' service to the Kings Head which was abandoned after only three months. (R.T. Wilson)

Opposite above: Parked outside Lennon Brothers, Wholesale Factors and General Importers, is a city-bound bus working on the 52 route from the Beeches Estate off Walsall Road. Although the bus has a number of passengers on board, it is without a driver and conductor as the bus is waiting for a crew change from the nearby Miller Street garage. Behind the bus is the Newtown Palace Bingo Hall. The parked bus is a Guy 'Arab' IV 6LW with a 27ft 6in long MCCW H30/25R body. This bus entered service from Miller Street on 4 July 1953 when it was of the vehicles replacing the city's final tramcars on the Erdington group of routes. It was still garaged at Miller Street when this photograph was taken in about 1964. (D.R. Harvey Collection)

Opposite below: The Newtown Palace had opened as a theatre just before the First World War on 5 January 1914 with a full-sized stage, but was soon converted into a cinema. It closed as a cinema on 22 April 1962 and was converted to a bingo hall, finally closing some twenty-one years later.

Above and below: The two bicycles parked outside A.W. Saywell's Rudge cycle dealership in the top photograph (F.N. Lloyd Jones) must have been 'the bee's knees' in 1949 as they were fitted with dropped handlebars. Car 579, a 1914-vintage United Electric Car Co. sixty-two seat bodywork with Brush-built Burnley maximum traction bogies is about to pass by the cycle shop. Just to the right of the tram is the entrance to Miller Street with tram tracks turning off Newtown Row so that trams could gain access to the tram depot. On the corner of Miller Street was the Thornton Restaurant and Milk Bar which had the grid effect window. This 40hp tram, equipped with Dick Kerr DK 13A motors, was fully enclosed in the late 1920s. Tram 579 had arrived at Miller Street after the closure of the Stratford Road group of tram routes in January 1937 and remained there until the final day of operation on 4 July 1953.

Looking back towards the city centre, tram tracks lead off Newtown Row into Miller Street towards the tram depot. Hidden by the tram is New John Street West, while marked by the Belisha Beacon on the left is New John Street. To the right of the tram is another row of shops including yet another tobacconists. Travelling towards Newtown and Perry Barr on the 6 route is car 18, one of the original class known as the 'Old' or 'Aston' bogies which had entered service in January 1904 with an open-top body. Subsequently fitted with top covers in July 1907, they were too tall at 16ft 3in to pass beneath the railway bridge at Aston Station and so spent the rest of their long lives on the Perry Barr service. Car 18 is being followed by a war-time Bedford OYD 3-ton lorry with a military-style bonnet, while parked on the left is an Austin and beyond that is a parked Standard Flying Eight Saloon.

The piano and gramophone dealers Warners at No. 145 Newtown Row near to Miller Street in about 1950. Notice the innovative for their time large plate-glass windows and the lighting. This publicity photograph was taken to promote the Birmingham Lighting Co. who provided the lighting which was kept on at nights. In the 1930s, old-timers recall that you could hire a piano from Warners for 1s 6d a week so marking yourself as a cut above the neighbours.

Miller Street tram depot. Miller Street was Birmingham Corporation Tramways first tram depot and was opened for the first tram route between Steelhouse Lane and the Aston UDC boundary at Aston Brook Street on 4 January 1904. The depot was a mere five tram tracks wide but was extended three times in the following years and eventually had a capacity for about 112 trams. The first open-top trams, bogie cars 1-20, spent nearly their whole lives working from this depot. After they were top-covered in 1907, cars 1-20 were almost entirely used on the Perry Barr service because their increased height precluded their use beyond the railway bridge at Aston Station Railway bridge. This is why they were so well photographed in Newtown Row! The six which survived the bombing of Miller Street in the night of 9 April 1941, when a total of twenty-four tramcars were destroyed, continued to operate until New Year's Eve 1949 when the 6 route was closed. With Newtown Row in the background, Miller Street survived to become the last operational depot on the Birmingham tram system, closing on Saturday 4 July 1953. On Thursday 25 June 1953, the workmen are trying to convert the depot for the new buses with the trams still operating around them. The first tram on the left is car 650, of 1923-vintage. This was one of the first twenty-five totally-enclosed bogie cars in the fleet and was destined to spend its entire forty-year life based at Miller Street. To the right is car 597, destined to be the last tram to be cut up, and 729 and 726 all waiting to take up their next duty, but there wouldn't be too many more to do. (C.A.S. Honnor)

Opposite above: On the right is St Stephen's church which was built in an Early English style in brick and sandstone. It was consecrated in 1844 and was at the centre of religious life in the Newtown area for over a century. Passing along Newtown Row travelling northwards towards Perry Barr is a City of Birmingham Tramways' steam tram and trailer. The steam tram service began operation on 25 November 1884 and continued until New Year's Eve 1906. Nicknamed 'shufflers' because of the shuffling gait caused by the pushing of their outside cylinders, the steam tram is a much maligned beast as it brought the first reliable public transport to a lot of people in the late nineteenth century. (D.R. Harvey Collection)

Working on the 6 route opposite St Stephen's church in 1949 is car 3 which was one of the six 1–20 class survivors of the war-time bombings. The church was closed for demolition early in 1950 just a few months after the closure of the trams. Newtown Row begins to drop down a gently sloping valley side towards the culverted crossing point of Aston Brook. Beyond the Austin Seven car and the distant tram is the just discernible Aston Hippodrome. (F.N. Lloyd Jones)

Above: Newtown Row was first mentioned in the 1780s and, as Aston grew larger in the early decades of the nineteenth century, so it expanded on to the higher ground to the west which lay along the road to Perry Barr and Walsall. Thus by the 1830s, Aston's Newtown area was being developed and some of the better quality terraces, distinguished by their heavily pedimented windows, lay in what was to become Newtown Row in the vicinity of St Stephen's church. Later as plots of land became more expensive and less available, the housing changed from cramped but still with vestiges of architectural style to jerry-built back-to-back houses around tiny cramped courtyards where water was raised from the same water source which also carried the excrement from as many as 200 people sharing a couple of earth closets. No wonder these houses were unhygienic and a source of typhoid and cholera! Car 452 is travelling along Newtown Row when working on the 6 route to Perry Barr. This tram was one of the pair of ex-CBT eight-wheeled trams which because of their length of 34ft 8in were nicknamed 'the Titanics'. They could always be distinguished as they were the only Corporation tramcars to have five side windows in each saloon. Number 451 is about to pass the junction with Cowper Street. This street was named after one William Cowper who was an early seventeenth-century ironmaster. (T.J. Edgington)

Opposite above: Newtown Row garage. The British Lion, a gents' hairdressers and an off-licence crowd together in this stretch of Newtown Row on 12 April 1960.

Opposite below: Work on Newtown Row on 18 January 1967 building what is to become a highway out of the city, taking traffic as quickly as possible towards Walsall and Sutton. The view looks towards Barclays Bank on the corner of Milton Street, a rather too grand building for the district until you realise that it was not local residents who were the bank's chief customers but local businesses and shopkeepers. Until the Municipal bank opened in Summer Lane in 1924 the Barclays Bank was the only bank in Newtown. William Cowper School is on the left.

Looking from High Street into a dingy-looking Newtown Row, two totally enclosed bogie cars pass each other when working on the 6 route, with the one on the left, inbound to the city, identifiable as car 579. This tram has just left the section of interlaced track, visible in the foreground, which ran from Phillips Street with a branch of Timothy White and Taylor on its far corner to just outside the House That Jack Built department store about 100 yards away. Opposite the chemist's shop on the left is a branch of George Baines, a good quality baker who had no less than thirty-four retail outlets which were all on the north side of Birmingham. On the right is Inkerman Street, another Newtown street named after a battle in the Crimean War. The Battle of Inkerman was fought on 5 November 1854, and was the principal land battle of the Crimean War of 1854–56. According to contemporary reports 'Generals fought like colonels, colonels fought like private soldiers and privates fought like heroes', and at a terrible cost, the British and French armies defeated the Russians. (D.R. Harvey Collection)

Opposite above: Spilsburys' pawnbrokers on the corner of Newtown Row and Cowper Street.

Opposite below: Work building the new Perry Barr Expressway, better known as the A34, on 22 May 1967. This Public Works Department photograph shows progress on the new road but also what was to be swept away, an array of well-loved buildings on this part of Newtown Row, including the Dog and Duck and The House That Jack Built.

The narrow section of High Street, Newtown meant that the tram track was interlaced and was effectively single line working. With the Aston Hippodrome in the background, a Fordson E83A van keeps well into the left as tramcar 451 travels towards it on its way into Birmingham on 6 July 1948. On the right, behind the cyclist, is a 1939 SS Jaguar. This lovely motorcar is passing The House That Jack Built, a high quality store which had the distinction of being the only independently-owned suburban departmental store in Birmingham. It had this single row of premises from 166-174 High Street. On the extreme right is Phillips Street with the aforementioned George Baines's shop on the corner, but next to it, also with the canvas blind pulled out, is a branch of Bywaters, who were pork butchers and made the most wonderful meat and pork pies. The man walking in the sun on the left has resisted the temptation of 'going for a quick one' in the Dog and Duck pub which was an Ansells house. It had a strange mixture of architectural styles with a touch of Arts and Crafts, seventeenth-century Dutch and windows with leaded Tudor-style lights. (D.R. Harvey Collection)

Tram 19, which was destroyed in an air-raid on Witton depot in December 1940, still sports flop-over destination boards as it stands between the Barton's Arms and the Globe Electric cinema at the bottom of High Street in about 1914. On the right is Newtown's third centre of culture. This was the Aston Hippodrome, which had been opened in 1908 with an auditorium capacity of 2,000. During this week, top of the bill was Edna Latonne, but second billing was Will Hay, (1888-1949), who would achieve greater stardom in his late 1930s films. (Commercial postcard)

High Street, Newtown in about 1908. Birmingham Corporation Tramways' double-decker, car 5 stands outside the Waggon and Horses public house on the corner of Webster Street. The tram is on its way from the short-lived Chain Walk terminus to Martineau Street. Three intrepid Edwardian lady cyclists are pedalling behind car 5, but are having to negotiate a parked barrow as well as avoiding the tram. The young woman in a dirty smock and the young lad in the foreground are standing at the corner of Burlington Street with the Aston Hippodrome immediately behind them. The large gabled buildings on the right which includes the double-fronted drapery shop owned by J.T. Powers are considerably newer than many of the surrounding properties in Newtown and date from the last decades of the nineteenth century. (J. Wybrow)

Virtually the same view about half a century later, with a considerable variety of shops including butchers, drapers and a tobacconists.

Tea dealers Asbury and Co. and George Holdens, at Nos 173 and 175 High Street between New Street and Inkerman Street around 1900.

Tram 677 picks up passengers as it travels on an outbound 6 service to Perry Barr. Car 677 was built in 1924 by the Brush Company of Loughborough and was mounted on EMB maximum traction bogies. This tram was one of forty in the 662-701 class, all of which spent their twenty-nine year lives based at Miller Street depot. The tram stands opposite the Bartons Arms at the corner of New Street. Just visible behind car 677 is the Globe Cinema, which had a distinctive globe above the entrance. This cinema had been opened in August 1913 and survived until September 1955. Coming down the hill from Park Lane in High Street is car 570, a UEC-built eight-wheeled tram which dated from 1914 and which originally had an open balcony. (F.N. Lloyd Jones)

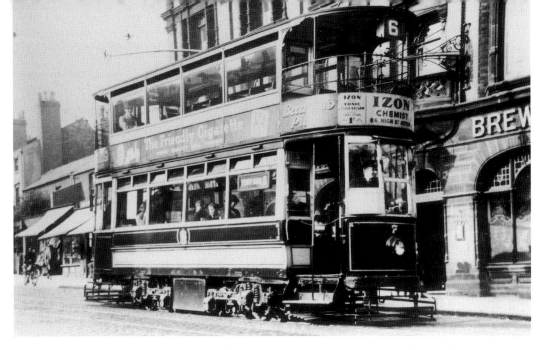

On 26 May 1939, a pristine-looking Aston Bogie, car 7, is travelling past the ornate exterior of the impressive Bartons Arms public house in High Street, Newtown. The tram looks good for a thirty-five year old vehicle, but alas not for much longer as it would be destroyed on the night of the 9-10 April 1941 when Miller Street depot was oil bombed. Of the twenty trams in the class, no less than thirteen were either destroyed or damaged beyond repair. The tram is travelling towards Birmingham when working on the 6 route. The advertisements being carried by the tram are redolent of another era with ones for Beecham's Pills and K4, 'The Friendly Cigarette', adorning, (or despoiling), the side of the tram. (L.W. Perkins)

In 1949, with cobbles still being the norm for most of Birmingham's streets, the last member of the 1-20 class of the original trams to work on the 6 route to Perry Barr, car 20, picks up passengers outside Tibble's gentlemen's tailors shop. Behind and to the left of the tram, where the 'Plywood Timber Mouldings' sign is located, were the premises of Ingall, Parsons and Clive who were coffin manufacturers. On the extreme right is the Globe Cinema while overtaking the tramcar is a Morris-Commercial CV 5-ton lorry. (R.T. Wilson)

Above: The city-bound tramcar working on the 6 route is dropping off its passengers in High Street, Six Ways at the Park Lane junction where the Inner Circle bus route crossed to go into Whitehead Road. Behind the pedestrians is Izon's dispensing chemist shop while on the extreme left is Herbert Toon's tobacconists. On the far corner of Park Lane, before High Street plunges down the steep hill towards the Bartons Arms, occupying the three-storied (*c.* 1860) premises is Beckett's dry-cleaners shop. The silver studs set into the road indicate a Belisha Beacon pedestrian crossing. These were named after the Minister of Transport, Leslie Hore Belisha who introduced them in 1934. There were no markings on the road surface until 1951 when Zebra Crossings were introduced. (R.T. Wilson)

Above: The driver of the tram is making some sort of mechanical adjustment to the tram loco as it stands in High Street, Six Ways. At the rear of the double-deck trailer, the tram's conductor looks on anxiously as the repair progresses. The tram displays the route letter P for Perry Barr; all the tram routes were given letters but because of the levels of illiteracy at the time, the route letters and the background on which the destination letter was printed were given different colours so it didn't matter if you couldn't read. The stencil for the Perry Barr route was on a black ground. This was the oldest part of Aston Newtown and the houses and tenements behind the tram looking back to Whitehead Road, are some of the earliest, dating from the 1850s. Alongside the tram is the Six Ways Stores and at the front of the locomotive is a newsagent and tobacconist's shop. Outside the shop is a news hoarding which has on it 'Japan's terms of peace' which dates this to about the last couple of days of August 1905 when at American instigation the victorious Japanese agreed terms with the Russians after their defeat in the Russo-Japanese War. (D.R. Harvey Collection)

Opposite below: In Park Lane when working on an Inner Circle 8 route. This AEC Regent 661 model with an English Electric H27/21R body is travelling towards High Street from Aston Cross where it will cross the No. 6 tram route and turn into Whitehead Road before heading off towards Hockley. The bus entered service in September 1930 and would be one of the last survivors of the 'piano-front' buses, where the upper front deck was set back from the top of the driver's cab. The bus is being followed by a 1936 Morris Ten-Four. On the left is Potters Hill and the first bus stop on the Inner Circle in Park Lane after leaving High Street, near Six Ways. No doubt Millington's butcher's shop would gain from the passing trade from people getting off the bus. The shop is selling British meat at between 3d and 1s, though without refrigerated counters, modern-day health and safety officials would have a field day.

The view as the Perry Barr Expressway is being built, looking down towards the Bartons on 22 May 1967.

Another one of the 1914-built UEC-bodied trams, car 583, stands in High Street, Six Ways on a gloomy day in the winter of 1949. As the tram is overtaken by a somewhat smoky lorry, it has just dropped off its passengers outside the Royal Exchange public house which dated from the 1840s. The tram has just passed one of the Salvage Department's battery electric dustcarts. This Birmingham manufactured Morrison Electricar DV4-type vehicle was built in 1940 and worked for nearly twenty-five years around the city's streets. Birmingham had the largest fleet of battery-electric dustcarts in the UK and between 1918 and 1971 operated a total of 262 vehicles. (R.T. Wilson)

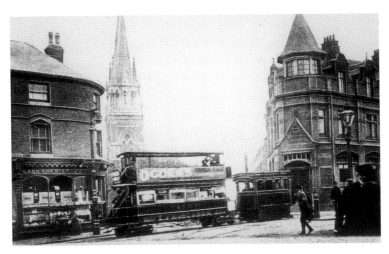

The steam-tram service through Newtown was the first to be operated by CBT and ran between Old Square in the town centre and Perry Barr just beyond the Birchfield Road depot at the junction with Witton Lane. This service continued until 31 December 1906 when the CBT lease expired and the route was taken over by the municipality on the following day having been converted to an electric tramway. Initially this new electric service only went as far as Newtown Row as legal disputes prevented a through service to Perry Barr which did not begin until 8 December 1909. Standing at Six Ways, Aston, with Victoria Road beyond the steam tram locomotive, the tram is on its way to Newtown and Birmingham. Behind the tram is Witton Road whose entrance is between Gash's Chemist shop and Christ Church Baptist Chapel on the left. The church had been built in the 1860s and after many years of dereliction is now fitted out as luxury flats. (D.R. Harvey Collection)

One of the 'Titanic' twins, car 451, the former CBT open-topper 178, is about to rattle over the somewhat worn-looking Lozells tram tracks at Six Ways, Aston in the shadow of the extravagantly Dutch-gabled National Provincial Bank. The Lozells to Gravelly Hill service was Birmingham's only inter-suburban tram route, opening on 7 May 1906 and being operated by the CBT Company until the service was taken over by the Corporation on 1 January 1912. Becoming the 5 route, it outlasted the Perry Barr service by some nine months only being closed on the last day of September 1950. On the corner of High Street and Alma Street is the Royal Exchange public house. The tramcar is working towards Perry Barr on the 6 service during 1949. Coming out of Victoria Road is an Austin 16 first registered in June 1947, while behind the tram is an Austin K3 lorry and behind that, almost at the same spot as the steam tram is yet another Austin, this time a Three-Way 30cwt van.

It would appear that the building on the corner of Witton Road and Birchfield Road had been a chemist's shop since the days of the steam trams when Mr Gash was the chemist. This impressive shop was diagonally opposite the Royal Exchange public house and by 1949 was known as Hedges Corner after the Birmingham-based dispensing chemist who, including this shop at No. 1A Birchfield Road, had 187 other branches in the city. As the three-wheeled Scammell Mechanical Horse comes across Six Ways from Victoria Road, car 13 has passed Hedges' shop and is waiting for a clear road before crossing Six Ways as it travels towards Birmingham and its city centre terminus in Martineau Street. On the left and partially hidden by the flat-bed lorry, is a war-time Midland Red double-decker bus which is coming out of Alma Street on its way to either Sutton Coldfield or Walsall. (R.T. Wilson)

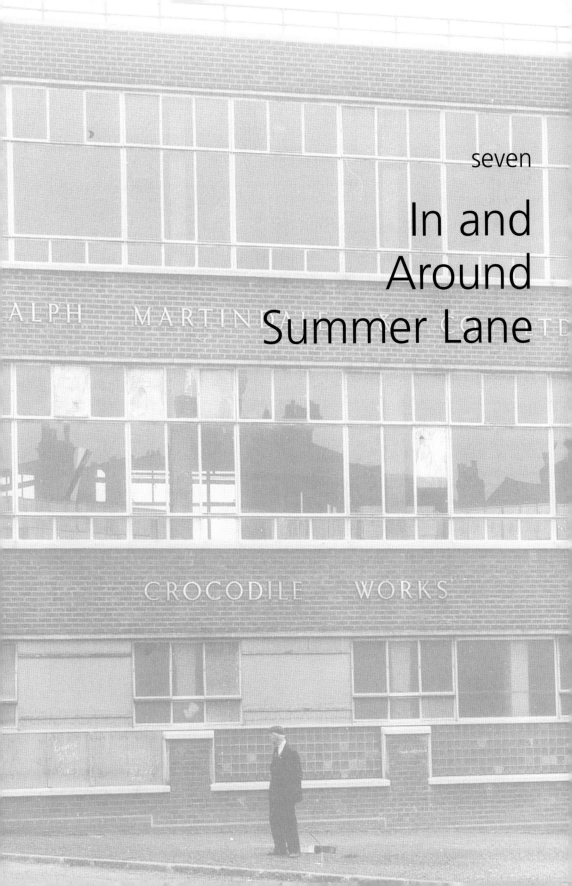

seven

In and Around Summer Lane

Above and below: Views of the shops at the bottom of Summer Lane which seem somehow to have survived all the redevelopment around them and now give a slight flavour of what the road must have looked like up to the 1950s. The top photograph is from around 1971, the bottom showing hopeful signs of repair work, from 2006.

Above: The Centro building in Summer Lane in 2006. (Ebenoes)

Below: A familiar site on the corner of Summer Lane and Loveday Street is White's ironmongers, and still trading. In the 1930s Mr White was remembered as always wearing a black skull cap and for being able to find a particular item from a stock that all seemed to consist of small packages, occupying every nook and cranny of the shop. The firm was established in 1849 and promoted itself as 'The Old Firm'.

The early days of the Unity Social Club on the corner of Summer Lane and New Summer Street. This illustration comes from the local magazine *Birmingham Faces and Places* volume 5, 1892. The accompanying article states that the club is 'undoubtedly the largest of its kind in the city. Moreover it fulfils a double purpose, for while it is intended for social reunions, one of its primary objectives is to encourage thrift among the working classes'. It had 3,800 members at this date and its facilities included excellent card rooms, a billiards and bagatelle room, a reading room and a lecture hall.

A wonderful photograph but difficult to identify accurately, It may be a funeral procession in Summer Lane.

A view along Summer Lane in July 1971 showing some redevelopment still to take place beyond the Royal George pub.

The CWU building in Summer Lane in 2006. Other prominent office buildings along Summer Lane include the main offices of the *Big Issue* and a martial arts centre. During the day the road tends to be reasonably busy but very quiet in the evenings, in contrast to what older residents might think of its heyday in the 1930s and immediately post-war.

In West Midlands PTE days, a former Birmingham City Transport vehicle, 2966, (JOJ 966), a Guy 'Arab' IV with an MCCW body is working on its way into the city on the 7 route during 1974. The bus has just passed by the large 1960s Duke of Quebec public house and is alongside the premises of the Birmingham Settlement. (D.R. Harvey)

Being overtaken by a City of Birmingham Bedford J1 ambulance, which has just left the ambulance station in Loveday Street, is 3127, (MOF 127). This 1953-vintage Crossley-bodied Daimler CVG6 is working on the 5 route to Court Lane, Perry Common and is travelling northwards along Summer Lane when in WMPTE ownership in 1974. On the left is the original Victorian boundary wall of the Birmingham Settlement. Behind the bus is Tower Street and on its corner is the round-ended Barrel Inn. (D.R. Harvey)

Freshly laid pavements and newly planted saplings on the corner of Theodore Street denote that the redevelopment of the Newtown area was well underway by 1965. Mr Hughes's newsagents and tobacconists shop is still trading in the back-to-back three-storey property which faces on to Summer Lane. Although the buildings on the extreme left behind the Austin A40 Farina and the brand-new Vauxhall Viva HA cars have already got DANGER notices on the boarded-up windows, the round-topped entry arch to the courtyard of this particular block of back-to-backs can be identified. In this courtyard there were nine properties which backed up to the factory wall of one of the many steel pen manufacturers who thrived in the area until the late inter-war period. This block of Victorian slums was between the distant Bridge Street West and New John Street West which the bus will shortly cross. Both the 5 and the 7 bus routes to and from Perry Common, respectively, used Summer Lane, by way of Loveday Street, Alma Street, Six Ways and Witton Road. The 5 route was introduced on 7 June 1926 and when the city to Portland Road route, given the number 7, was introduced on 26 September 1927, the two routes were combined to form a west to north cross-city bus route. It was nearly always a double-deck operated route, but somehow one of Perry Barr garage's single-deckers, 2239, (JOJ 239), a Leyland 'Tiger' PS2/1 with a Weymann front-entrance 34-seater body, had strayed on to the 5 route showing Birmingham's infamous SERVICE EXTRA destination display. On the sky-line, representing the new Central Development Area of Newtown, are two of the multi-storey blocks of flats which had been built overlooking the underpass on the A34 at Six Ways. (L. Mason)

Above: Virtually the same spot as on the previous page but forty years later with the flats at Lount Court on the left.

Left: This photograph is included to show how the building of the Middleway had an effect on the Summer Lane environment and the local communities, even making walking from one end of Summer Lane to the other a less than inspiring journey.

The Crocodile Works at the Summer Lane, Porchester Road, Alma Street junction. It is currently, like many of the older factories in the area, under threat of demolition. This photograph was taken in April 1962. For many years the factory belonged to Ralph Martindale and Co., manufacturers of edged tools.

Above: Mott Street, showing a variety of workshops, the most prominent being the stampers and dyers, E.H. Whitehouse.

Below: A view of Nos 229-231 Brearley Street showing the premises of the builder's merchants H.E. Appleby and Co. in October 1858.

Above and below: How the area gradually deteriorated. Two views of Brearley Street; the earlier one taken in October 1958 showing the premises of Shorthouse Body fittings, which were at 256-260, next door to a money-lending office and an electroplaters.

A view down Inkerman Street on 11 April 1960 as the road falls into disrepair. At the bottom of the street Aston High Street and the Dog and Duck pub are just about visible. All of this scene was to be swept away.

Nos 64-74 Porchester Street on 26 September 1966.

Asylum Road on 24 November 1960. The road was named after 'The Asylum' which was one of the few buildings in this part of Aston in the early nineteenth century. It was a children's home, for the infant poor, run under the auspices of the Guardians. In 1818 there were 380 children living there, 300 who worked on making pins, straw plait and lace. The Asylum closed in 1846 and thereafter such children went to the Birmingham workhouse in Winson Green and the Summer Lane buildings were demolished in about 1875. This view shows how houses and courtyards would be intermingle with small shops and how difficult it would have been to either renovate buildings or even partly redevelop the area.

The corner of Great Russell Street and New John Street West on a summer's day in 1959 with one of the many corner shops, in this instance, advertising fruit and vegetables.

Another corner shop on Great Russell Street, this time the Brearley Street corner. A young lad waits for his mum to come out of the Victory fish and chip shop on a November afternoon in 1960 and probably hoping she has remembered to ask for some 'scratchings'. You can virtually smell the salt and vinegar and taste the Vimto.

The aftermath of a German bomb. Inspecting the damage to houses in Bridge Street West after a raid on 30 July 1942. Newtown suffered heavily from bombing because of the number of important factories in the district. This also meant that once the war ended and lives returned to normal the area looked even more depressing and squalid than it had done previously and soon led to plans for wholesale redevelopments which were to change Newtown's look and character dramatically.

Another street which was suffering from age and planning blight, Milton Street on a February day in 1960. The photo shows Nos 3-9.

Porchester Street with the courts leading up to the Porchester Arms at the top of the road. The photograph was taken by the city's Public Works Department on 26 September 1961.

Alma Street, November 1960. Alma Street got its name from the Battle of Alma which took place during the Crimean War on 20 September 1854. By the date of this view Alma Street had some pretty appalling back-to-back courtyards such as Myrtle, Victoria, Builth and Roslin Places, which despite their attractive names, were brick-floored courtyards with communal outside lavatories and washing lines criss-crossing the dingy and unhealthy areas. The 33 bus route to Kingstanding went from the city centre by way of Summer Lane, Alma Street to Six Ways, Aston until the 6 tram route was abandoned on New Year's Eve 1949. In this view a 1719, (HOV 719), a Leyland 'Titan' PD2/1 with a fifty-four-seater body built by Brush of Loughborough, has just passed into Alma Street, from Six Ways, on 15 December 1949. The bus is alongside the Royal Exchange public house, which occupied the imposing corner site between Alma Street and High Street, Six Ways. Parked on the left is a Chrysler DeLuxe Eight which has a 1935 Middlesex registration. (G.F. Douglas, courtesy A.D. Packer)

Opposite: The redevelopment of the district in the 1960s and 1970s has altered some of the roads and road layouts but the above map illustrates how Newtown was laid out when most of the photographs in this book were taken.

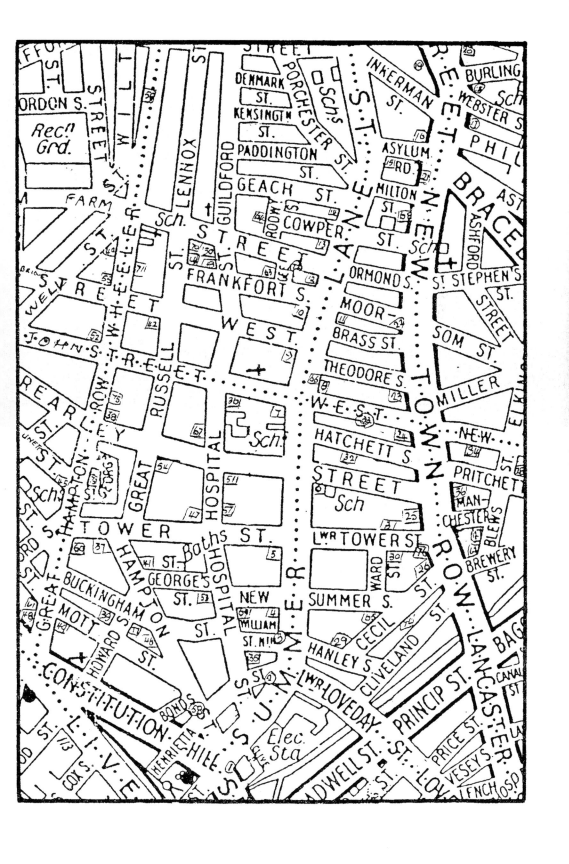

An aerial photo of the Newtown area taken on 26 May 1967. The two main roads which define Newtown's character, Newtown Row and Summer Lane run horizontally through the view. The Bartons Arms is down in the bottom right hand corner just above the plane's wing while across the road the new Newtown shopping centre is under

construction along with the Perry Barr expressway. The scope of the Crocodile works is clearly evident across the road from the shopping centre. However there is still enough of the nineteenth-century housing visible to show just how dramatic was to be the redevelopment for the lives of the people of Newtown.

Other local titles published by Tempus

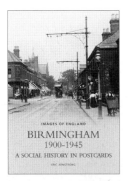

Birmingham A Social History in Postcards
ERIC ARMSTRONG

This fascinating collection of over 200 archive postcards provides a nostalgic insight into the changing history of Birmingham over the period 1990-1945. For over a quarter of this time Britain was at war and the political and social changes felt were immense, not least in Birmingham, a major industrial city. This book will awaken memories of a bygone time for all those who worked or lived in this vibrant community.

0 7524 4037 3

Central Birmingham Pubs
JOSEPH MCKENNA

This fascinating volume records the pubs, inns, taverns and beerhouses of the central city, an area now within the present Inner Ring road and the Bull Ring. This is the very heart of the city and although it comprises only one square mile and can be crossed on foot in less than half an hour, it is an area that has seen over 760 pubs – all of which are faithfully recorded here.

0 7524 3873 5

Haunted Birmingham
ARTHUR SMITH AND RACHEL BANNISTER

From creepy accounts of the city centre to phantoms of the theatre, haunted pubs and hospitals, *Haunted Birmingham* contains a chilling range of ghostly phenomena. Drawing on historical and contemporary sources, you will hear about a landlady who haunts the site of her death, the two workmen who died during the building of the Town Hall, the late mayor who still watches over the city, the last man publicly hanged in Birmingham, and many more ghostly goings-on.

0 7524 4017 9

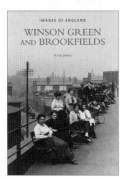

Winson Green and Brookfields
PETER DRAKE

This book provides a fascinating look at an area which came into being following the opening of Matthew Boulton's great Soho manufactory and remained relatively rural until the mid-nineteenth century, when Birmingham Town Council found sites for a new Borough Prison and workhouse. For much of its short history it suffered from the consequences of the industrial development that brought it into existence. This photographic record pays tribute to the people who grew up and worked in this tough but close community.

0 7524 3049 1

If you are interested in purchasing other books published by Tempus, or in case you have difficulty finding any Tempus books in your local bookshop, you can also place orders directly through our website
www.tempus-publishing.com